What readers are

"Personalities in the Pulp

"If you are well into your career you will put your own names on Jim's characters. If you are just starting, recognize and use Jim's characters to be successful"

Michael A. Roberts
Executive Director
Washington Pulp and Paper Foundation
Seattle, Washington

"A great guide full of useful information written in a fun style for those of us who like to learn the 'science and art of personality impact.'"

Jack Bray
Vice President, Manufacturing Operations
Domtar
Fort Mill, South Carolina

"I heartily endorse your new book outlining the leadership characteristics of paper business management..."

Jim Painter[1]
Vice President and General Manager, Retired
Mount Juliet, Tennessee

---

[1] Jim had a lot more to say...you can find it at the end of this book.

a

"If you have elected a career in manufacturing lots of people may give you advice. When new, almost everyone, given a little encouragement, has some. Most is worth hearing as those giving it, whether colleagues or managers, are sharing a lot about themselves. Good advice has to be sorted out, especially in the context of your responsibilities to your employer, your family and yourself. Doing this with the right guidelines helps you as much with understanding the people you work with, as much as with controlling your own behaviour. Both are essential to effectively meeting your combined responsibilities.

"My best source for such guidelines is Jim Thompson, who I've known for about a decade. In this book, he again puts forward the standards for behaviour, starting with integrity. Then, through example, he covers most of the personalities that create problems in all industries, not just pulp and paper, although we seem to have enough for all. He rounds it off with responses based on the fundamental guidelines. I frequently recommend Jim's columns to colleagues and clients. This book I shall be giving to young people entering our industry."

Dene H. Taylor, Ph.D.
President
SPF – Inc.
New Hope, Pennsylvania

b

"Jim Thompson is a true class act who sets a high bar not only for himself, but for those with whom he engages, personally and professionally. Throughout my twenty + years of doing business with Jim, I was able to gain extensive and invaluable knowledge. Jim's integrity, work ethic and honorable nature makes him far more than 'just a business colleague'; Jim is instead a trusted mentor, an industry leader and an unrivaled friend."

Ed Kersey
General Manager
Pratt Paper (LA), LLC
Shreveport, Louisiana

"Space is not the final frontier, people are! This book is a great insight into the workings and people of our very complex industry."

Ed Graf
Industry Consultant
Washington Island, Wisconsin

"Jim's observations on our industry are honest to the point where we can each learn from them. He truly "calls 'em as he sees 'em" and he covers each personality with the understanding that comes from experience. A great read. Take notes."

Jon Kerr
Senior Consultant
Fisher International
Loveland, Ohio

"Insightful, heartfelt, a recommended read for the industry veteran, as well as the industry novice"

Jay Hennessey
Mill Manager
Pratt Paper Indiana
Valparaiso, Indiana

"I believe the unfortunate aspect of Jim's new book is the people that should read it are not the ones who will read it. And the ones who do read it are the ones you want spinning the invoice printer in your mill. I also agree the centering thought is the <u>centering thought</u>!"

Gary W. Nyman
SME Innovative Solutions
International Paper-Technology
Chapin, South Carolina

"Sage advice and worthwhile considerations for young professionals as well as thoughtful observations and motivation for the seasoned veteran. Thanks for doing what you do, and sharing your thoughts. You are candid…. the real deal."

Jeff Smith
Account Manager
BTG Americas, Inc.
Atlanta, Georgia

Personalities in the Pulp & Paper Industry

the 6-ton elephant in the room no one talks about

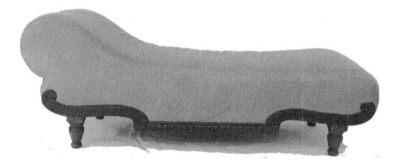

by

Jim Thompson

Second Edition, June 2017

ISBN 978-0999123409

This book is dedicated to

Elliott F. Winton, M.D.

and

Jessica J. Neely, P.A.

of

The Winship Cancer Institute

Emory University

Atlanta, Georgia

who through unbelievable and extraordinary

competence,

experience, and energy,

in harmony with our Almighty Creator,

have kept me alive for 17 years and counting

in my battle against Non-Hodgkin's Lymphoma

Other books by Press Nip Impressions, Duluth, Georgia, USA

On Employment (2004)

The Osage Mill (2005)

The Pulp and Paper Industry: a perspective for

Wall Street (2006)

The Lazy Project Engineer's Path to Excellence (2006)

Raising EBITDA: the lessons of Nip Impressions (2014)

Advertising Arguments 2015 (2015)

Advertising Arguments 2016 (2016)

(indicates first printing)

Contents

Prelude

My formal introduction to the pulp and paper industry started in the mid-1970's at Procter & Gamble in Cincinnati, Ohio. Ten years before that, I was helping my dad cut pulpwood on our family farms in Highland County, Ohio. At that time, the pulpwood went to the Mead Paper Company in Chillicothe, Ohio. As we labored under the almost completely manual work of those days, I was determined to never join this industry. Well, sometimes we are wrong, aren't we? When I was looking at the pulp and paper industry from the end of a chain saw, cant hook, and log chain, it did not look so good. When I got inside, I was really hooked.

Over the years, I have worked as an employee of pulp and paper companies (machinery designer, project engineer, process engineer, mill manager), as a consultant, both with Jaakko Pöyry and operating my own companies, as a banker's engineer, structural steel detailer, expert witness, a manufacturer's representative, advertising agency principal, public company board of director's member, founder of a small non-profit institute and as a trade publication media company owner in the industry. It is fair to say I have seen it all.

Despite all of this, it is remarkably noticeable that the personalities of the people that make up this industry are seldom discussed except on an ad hoc basis.

At the end of the day, however, the industry's individual successes and failures are largely attributable to personalities. Yes, we can blame the Internet for killing publishing grades or foreign buyers for distorting the waste paper and pulp markets, but the individual successes and failures of distinct facilities have almost exclusively been personality driven.

Let's face it, we are all "nuts" whether or not we have chosen this industry for our career. The good news is we are not alone—the world is completely full of dysfunctional people, some more so, some less so, but we all have our share of quirks. The psychology and psychiatry professions have attempted to describe us all, irrespective of our avocation or profession and whether we reached our current status through environment or heredity. I highly recommend you familiarize yourself with their reference volume. It is called the Diagnostic and Statistical Manual of Mental Disorders. The latest version as of this writing is "5." For those in the know, the shorthand name is "DSM-5." You may want to start by reading up on it in Wikipedia, but I highly recommend you eventually buy a copy for yourself.

Some may think a book with a title such as the one here should delve into the intricacies of the application of the famous Myers-Briggs test or other such matters. You can stop reading now if that is what you seek. We'll not go there; this will be an interpretation of all that I have seen in over forty-five years in industry with references to standardized tests lightly covered near the end.

Section I—Framing the Subject

Chapter 1—Interests, Aptitude, Personality, and Family

Whatever you are doing today, it is most likely you were drawn or driven to it by interests you developed in your formative years, an aptitude you have, your personality, and, to wrap it all up, your family history. You may be very bright, average or a learning challenged person—these measurable traits will come out in one of the four qualities listed in the chapter title. In fact, we will see as this book progresses that your IQ has little to do with your success.

Now, we will take the attributes in reverse order from the above, for the reverse order is somewhat how these issues will develop for most people (but not how they will play out in their lives).

———

Your family experiences have a great deal to do with what you decide to do in your adult life. If you grew up in a difficult and perhaps even a substance abusing environment, you may choose to follow that path, or, some spark may have inspired you to break out and go a different direction. Social workers around the world would like to find that "some spark" and turn it on in many, many children. It remains elusive.

We find many people, especially in the hourly ranks, that grew up in a family that worked in pulp and paper mills who choose to do the same themselves. Whether this is an exhibition of lack of ambition or a clinging to the comfortable, each case must be interviewed to ascertain the reason for the choice. However, given the 24/7 nature of paper mill operations, it is remarkable that any choose to join our industry having grown up with parents on odd shifts, with weekends and holidays being interrupted, and other intrusions not considered part of "normal life" by most. Yet they continue coming to the mill generation after generation.

I mentioned the hourly ranks, but this holds true in the salaried ranks as well. I know many second-generation professionals and a few third-generation professionals active in our industry to this day.

On the opposite side of the coin, if you grew up in a family of, shall I say, rabid, environmentalists, it is highly likely your family predisposition will be a strong force in preventing you from even considering the pulp and paper industry as a viable career choice unless you just happen to be a rebel. It would take an exceptional high school science teacher or some other such personal intervention for you to consider anything outside the comfort zone of your family. By the way, this is not your fault or your family's fault—it is the fault of an industry that came very late to the idea of public relations.

And then there is the reality that a person may have never been exposed to the pulp and paper industry. This is ironic, for the very first thing put on their bottom was a diaper with a strong pulp component and likely the very first thing that touched their nose was a tissue. However, pulp and paper products are so ubiquitous that 99% of the population never give them a thought.

Of course, in the broadest sense, this entire book is about personalities, after all it is a key word in the title. Here we want to consider personalities in a slightly narrower way.

For most of its existence, the pulp and paper industry has tended to attract personalities that can best be described in the popular colloquialism, "alpha male." Since the mid 1970's, just like in many other industries and professions, the gender and other personal attributes have been blurred a great deal (this is good), but the pulp and paper industry is not a homogenous monolith, so various corners of the industry tend to draw various personality types. We will talk about these in future chapters.

There is plenty of room in the industry for leaders, followers, the gregarious and the quiet loners. While there is no room for the lazy and the shirkers, the industry is large enough that many of these non-contributors have found places to hide.

Quick story. In the 1990's, as phone systems became more sophisticated and automated, it became popular to do away with real live receptionists in paper mill lobbies. They were replaced with a phone and a directory or simply the guard shack. The door into the offices was locked and someone on the inside had to come to the lobby to receive any visitors. On one hand, this made sense—seldom do customers come to mills and when they do, they are escorted around as if they are royalty. One fleet of operations where a friend of mine happened to be CEO did not follow the crowd and left their receptionists in place. I asked him why. Answer—we lose more money before noon through inefficient operations than it costs to keep a receptionist for a year. He was right. And now that he has retired, I am sure his successor has done away with the receptionists in all this company's facilities and I am sure they still lose more money before noon through inefficient operations than the receptionists used to cost them in a year. The shirkers and the slackers still have places to hide and bleed the industry of millions of dollars each year.

Today, there is room in the industry for more than the "alpha male." Many women have joined the industry and have risen to top positions of leadership and to seats on Boards of Directors. And the diversity goes far beyond just male and female. Although not quite as diverse perhaps as a fashion house in Paris, you will find the industry has embraced people of nearly all orientations and ethnicities.

We can say the pulp and paper industry has nearly all personalities found in the DSM-5 (see Prelude). In fact, I can't think of one it has missed.

———

Aptitude is defined as "a natural ability to do something" according to Google. I think this is universally understood. So, what aptitudes are necessary to have a pleasing career in the pulp and paper industry? If we are talking about operations, maintenance, or the technical department, one certainly needs to have a strong aptitude for mathematics and the sciences. Beyond mathematics and sciences, one needs to have a bit of mechanical aptitude, in fact, many mills today give mechanical aptitude tests as one of their screenings for new employees. To rise to positions of leadership, one will need strong leadership skills (although we have certainly seen many people rise to positions of leadership lacking these, often with disastrous results).

A predisposition for honesty, high ethical and moral values are keys to success. Yes, as unbelievable as it may seem to me, here in the early part of the twenty-first century it is necessary to state what should be obvious. There has been many a career cut short, indeed in a few cases mills closed, because the leadership did not have a strong sense of honesty and ethics. Moral missteps have been the end of many more careers.

Pulp and paper mills are very large and largely mechanical industrial behemoths. If you are not comfortable picturing yourself in such an environment or if you rub your hands with glee at the thought of the opportunities to rip off your employer in such a vast setting, you may want to look elsewhere to fulfill your lifelong dreams.

Those without aligned aptitudes are usually discovered eventually and leave the industry quietly after many years of struggle or dramatically when their malfeasance is finally discovered. You cannot change the industry in these basic areas—if you don't fit, the sooner you come to this realization the better for you.

———

Your interests are simple. What interest you and perhaps is something you would like to be associated with for the rest of your career? When I was in high school, it was obvious that I had a mechanical aptitude and I was interested in designing farm machinery. I started university to pursue a degree in mechanical engineering towards achieving that goal. A girl came along, I got married and (partially) forgot farm machinery. Then came an opportunity to discover paper machines. They were the biggest, most beautiful mechanical creatures I had ever seen. A lifelong love affair was kindled.

You may have more of a chemical bent, and with that, you too can fall in love with the pulp and paper industry. Manufacturing pulp, conveying it as a slurry and seeing it come out the other end as either baled pulp or a piece of paper or tissue is pretty fascinating stuff. Then there are the additive chemicals, biological considerations, the environmental operations and all else necessary for a modern operation.

In my lifetime, I have seen the mechanical and chemical operations of pulp and paper facilities go from the visual and atmospheric to the subatomic and pressurized, controlled environments. Controls have gone from simple mechanical valves and levers to sophisticated computer control. It has been quite a journey, not unlike those taken in any other industry.

Chapter 2—The effects of age and maturity

If you enter our industry, indeed any industry or profession, at a young age (let's say below thirty), you tend to look at all those with whom you come in contact as being wiser and more experienced than yourself. This is a general statement— maturity will temper your viewpoint, especially if you served in the military, were a member of the Greek community in college or perhaps played collegiate sports (let me hasten to say these three are not equal; they are merely grouped together here to imply that all impart a degree of maturity). These pre- employment opportunities will have given you the ability to look at people with a bit more introspection than that of a bright-eyed, naïve farm boy (me).

In other words, you tend to believe your coworkers if you are naïve. You may go as far as to hang on their every word. A caution—this is not wise. Draw on all your experiences, ask plenty of questions (mostly of yourself) and determine the degree of sanity that actually prevails in this new environment where you find yourself. Be especially watchful of the cynical oldster that wants to take you under their wing and show you "how things are done around here." They didn't know who you were last week, do you think they really have that great of an interest in you now? Of course not, they are just making sure you don't ask too many questions and upset the cozy little world they have created for themselves.

There is a story I have told several times about the first major engineering department in which I worked. It was huge— nearly 2,000 strong. In the end, my mother nailed it—she asked why this company would need such a large engineering department. In ten years, she was proven correct—it had been reduced to a mere shadow of its former self. Of course, when I joined it, I was gaga about the whole thing—its size, the projects it was working on, the obviously large expenditures that were approved to design machinery in-house that you could buy for half the price from suppliers. All of this was done in the name of quality and durability—as the company line went, no one could have our company's interests at heart as much as we did ourselves, could they? Quality takes time and money the delusion went on. It also helped that this department consisted almost entirely, I am convinced to this day, of people who had thrived on doing high school science fair projects. We had all found our home, we were delighted with it and couldn't see how anything could possibly be wrong with it. Except that it was a giant money sucking machine from another era, gone before my career was one fourth completed (but I had departed long before that).

So, you will join, at any age, a subgroup or department of people at an employer who thinks everything is just fine as it is and sees no reason to change. In fact, if you are brought in as a change agent, as soon as they discern this, they will fight you tooth and nail, do everything possible, ethical and unethical, to discredit you with the objective of throwing you out and making sure their world stays just like it was before you arrived. As you will find throughout this book, people have a strong desire to leave things as they are.

My observations are that those who have reached thirty years of age usually are no longer sucked in by the "magic" of big business. They have reached a level of maturity allowing them to understand that all is never as it seems, and what might be the stated purpose of their company or division, indeed whatever reason was given to even hire them, is only partially the truth. It is not that anyone tried to deceive them, although this has certainly happened in some cases, it is that the incumbents have been deceiving themselves every day for years. One who comes into such a situation with half decade or more of experience and a solid thinking ability sitting atop their shoulders will quickly discern the real from the delusional and modify their behavior accordingly. The finesse with which they modify their behavior will determine whether (a) they survive and (b) whether they become an effective change agent. More on this finesse later.

At the other end of the spectrum, I have seen, often common in aged forty-plus hires, who, through their experiences are so cynical, that even if the new environment is excellent and is on the move as a continuously improving entity, will sit back and immediately develop a defensive posture. They have been beat up for so long that the bright-eyed attitude of the twenty-five-year-old has been completely taken out of them, indeed, it is difficult to imagine they were ever of such an ilk.

We might as well stop right here and clear something up. For those of you who are familiar with my writings, you have been expecting this. For those of you who are not, let me introduce you to a concept that applies everywhere you ever go, any business, any non-profit, anywhere except government. That concept is this: every employee must exist to support "spinning the invoice printer." Today invoices are often electronic and never printed on paper, so the statement is obviously figurative. But think about it—no organization that is dependent on sales, and that includes every for-profit organization and non-profit (unless it is living off an endowment) organization must be focused on producing invoices. Rationally, they will produce invoices with the least possible effort (expenditures). So, the existence of humans in that organization (after all, humans are just a necessary evil in such an environment—they get sick, they sue their employers and so forth) must be because they are necessary to produce invoices. So, either you are involved in an activity that directly produces invoices or an activity necessary to produce invoices legally (a regulatory compliance function, for instance). Being involved in a regulatory compliance function that is not directly related to the production of the services or goods for which the entity is known is dangerous—you are subject to outsourcing every day you work there—outsourcing to an entity whose services that spin their invoice printer is providing regulatory guidance to those who have neither the time or expertise to do it themselves. Safety in employment is producing the good or service your company makes—everything else can be outsourced.

In summary for this chapter, I might say an organization is what it is. How you perceive it coming in the door is wholly dependent or your past experiences of lack of experiences and a good way to (albeit imprecisely) to measure this is by looking at your age when you cross the threshold to your new employer.

Chapter 3—The delusions of your employer

I was once working as an advertising agency principal with a large engineering company. The Senior Vice President asked me to come up with a new, catchy slogan for the company. After a bit of thought, I stole a slogan from *"Annie Get Your Gun."* I ran it by him and he heartily approved. He asked me to introduce it at a retreat for their senior executives.

Showing up at the retreat, I worked through the iterations that I had shown the Senior VP, and as the finale, introduced the slogan "Anything they can do [our great big engineering company] can do better." Immediately a senior operations manager protested that this was not true, that their competition was just as good as they were. The Senior VP, followed by me, jumped on him. Our admonishment was this: If you don't think you are working at the best company in the world doing what we are doing, you had better go find that company and seek employment there.

In another scenario, some years before the one described above, I was the Mill Manager in a decrepit old mill we were trying to "turn around" and save. The locals, third and fourth generation employees, did not understand. They would bring me yellowed old newspaper clippings from the 1940's (and this was in the '80's) that said such and such an improvement in this mill made it the leader in its field worldwide. Of course, those improvements had long since been eclipsed by the competition.

Every place of employment (and this does include government entities, unlike my exclusion of them in the last chapter) suffers from delusions as to its standing in the world in which it

11

competes and perhaps even in worlds where it doesn't think it competes.

This happened to newsprint and printing & writing papers in the 1990's and 2000's. They never had thought that this new thing called the Internet would nearly put them out of business. But it has. We never know where competition is coming from.

This happened to that engineering department in that large company that I mentioned earlier. Yes, we saw Computer Aided Design (CAD) coming but we foolishly thought this would give use more time to do our work—we were too blind to see it would take our jobs.

So, if we go back to my opening vignette in this chapter we find something that is true coupled with something that must be false for every entity except one in a given field. That is this: you must believe you work for the best company in your field, while at the same time you know only one company, by definition, can be the best company in your field. You would have to agree that the likelihood that you work for the best company in your field is very small, unless you are a monopoly. Thus, herein lies at least one delusion that rattles around inside that place you call your employer—you think you are the best, but are you really?

There can be holistic delusions and department by department delusions. These may be promulgated by grand slogans ginned up by public relations and human resource companies to inspire customers and employees. They may be developed by strong departmental leaders who see their job as making their corner of the company the best it can be. There may even be "urban legends" born of extraordinary events from years ago—events no current employee was witness to—that have been carried down through the decades as dogma, the origins of which no one questions.

Your job is simple to state and hard to do. Sort out the delusions, large and small, in the organization whose name is imprinted in the upper left-hand corner of your paycheck or deposit advice and then choose a path: flight or fight.

How do you sort out the delusions? Read everything you can find on your competitors, real and imagined. There is plenty of public information available to do this. Attempt to find the next "Internet" that may blindside your business (and it may come from almost any direction; for instance, if you are in the plastic bag business and the environmentalists say these are bad, you are toast).

Who is not a good source of information on the state of delusion at your employer? Your fellow employees, especially the ones who have been there for a long time. They are so steeped in the company mantra and legends that they have become polarized: either they think they do work for the best employer in their field or they have become so cynical that they are just praying for and counting the days until their retirement.

Once you have done the requisite study, you will need to make a decision: again, flight or fight. Flight is a noble course of action if you determine the organization is set in its ways, competition is on the horizon and you have neither the skills or position to affect the outcome, now or in the next few years. Fight is the noble course if you have been brought in at a level you can impact the organization and have the skills or can identify employees with the skills to make the changes necessary to assure success of the company.

Before we wrap this up, though, let me say delusions are not always bad. Exhibit One is a funny little bald man named Jeff Bezos. In the mid 1990's, he started an online bookstore, not much different from other online bookstores at the time. Today he is personally chasing the highest net worth person in the world, Exhibit Two, Bill Gates, who brazenly sold IBM a half-baked idea for a computer operating system a decade earlier than Bezos launched his business.

I am not making your delusion discernment any easier—what may look like a delusion to one person may prove otherwise eventually. However, since we are largely talking about established pulp and paper companies in the confines of this book, you'll likely find your job a bit easier than trying to find the next Amazon or Microsoft. And there is another important distinction. Both Bezos and Gates knew full well they were embarking on a highly risky path which might lead to great rewards or crashing to the ground. The delusions in established pulp and paper companies are often the result of employees afraid of change and hence following an equally risky narrative (but more likely a false one) than that pursued by a startup. Worse still, they don't even recognize the risk of their delusion because they can't allow themselves to think of the alternative should it be false.

This reaches all the way to the Board of Directors. There have been several pulp and paper companies disassembled by value seeking Wall Street activists in recent years precisely because the board was paralyzed, either due to ossification or embarrassment, when forced to self-assess their decisions over the past decade or longer. Delusion knows no rank, title or pay grade.

Chapter 4—The delusions of credentials

When I started extensively writing about this industry nearly two decades ago, one very senior, retired professor from a famous pulp and paper school wrote to me on at least two separate occasions. His missives went something like this: "How dare you write about the pulp and paper industry as if you are knowledgeable, you did not attend or graduate from [the school where he taught for over forty years]." Well, I did take a short course there one summer, but I doubt that would have impressed him if I had bothered to respond with that news. And, yes, my education is only a BS in Mechanical Engineering supplemented with all the coursework for a Masters in engineering economics. Perhaps I am not worthy.

Graduates from the school where he taught tend to be known throughout the industry for being a bit overly self-assured as to their competency. This was likely a somewhat valid and merited recognition when the industry was going through the period of great enlightenment and discovery of all things pulp and paper molecularly (a period I would define as approximately 1970 to 1990). However, today, such knowledge can be literally bought off the shelf while at the same time successfully operating a pulp and paper company has become far more complex. Many skills are needed today beyond how to disassemble a tree, bleach the fiber, and put it back together as a consumer product.

Yet, this school I am picking on is not alone in sending forth bright young graduates who think their education has prepared them for all that is necessary to be president of a pulp and paper company inside three weeks.

Their naïveté reminds me of the first day in algebra class when I was a freshman in high school. One kid raised his hand. When the teacher called on him he said, "I don't understand what we are going to do in this class, we explored mathematics quite extensively in the eighth grade." I have seen graduates from pulp and paper schools show up at their first job with similar attitudes.

In the last twenty-five years, I have spent a great deal of time and treasure supporting the many pulp and paper schools in the United States. To a school, every one of them says they are the greatest. Yet, just as we discovered in the last chapter, it is obvious that only one among many can be the best, all the others must fall behind the best. Granted, these schools tend to specialize a bit, so it might be fair to say one school is great at turning out graduates specializing in a certain niche while another turns out graduates specializing in another niche. Nevertheless, bright eyed graduates can show up for their first day of work thinking they are fully prepared to solve all their new employer's problems.

The inoculation against this over confidence phenomenon is summer jobs, internships, and co-op programs in the mills. I strongly encourage this, in fact, back to my own education, I had an excellent co-op experience which did much to prepare me for the workaday world.

Yet, all our new hires do not come from industry specific scholastic programs. What are other sources? The military academies have supplied many junior military officers (typical age—about 27 or 28) and we have hired many business school graduates, many with advanced degrees. Dare I say they may be cockier, more self-assured than the previously mentioned cadres? Why? I think most of these come into the industry with the idea this is a back water, antique industry and they are here to drag us kicking and screaming into the 21st century. Hence, they are often condescending and arrogant.

One final source of those with delusions about their credentials. They can come from a peer group company or from another facility within your own company. In the case where the facility where you work has a bad reputation within the company, "knights on white horses" from your sister facilities can be quite delusional about their skills and your need for their skills. It could be you need their skills, but when they come in with an attitude, you'll never get them, because you won't allow them to express them in a manner to which you are willing to listen.

As we have seen in the last two chapters, delusions abound from many sources. Delusions get in the way of seeking and maintaining excellence. This is true for the one administering help to a given situation as well as one receiving help from a particular person or entity. We have one more area of delusions to cover before we move on.

Chapter 5—The delusions of "free"

If you recall my previous discussion of "spinning the invoice printer" the obvious corollary to that is to produce the highest net profit among your peers. Thus, step one is to bring in as much revenue as you can and step two is retain as much as you can. Do that and you will be successful, or so people think. The stumble is in the execution and this involves more delusions.

First, there is the delusion that your suppliers are going to give you something or at least sell to you at a lower price than they sell to anyone else. Think about this for a minute. Do you not think their company has the same net profit objective as your company? Namely, to maximize their net profit? Do you see the word "free" or "giveaway" in there anywhere? Granted, when introducing a new product or protecting market share, you may get a deal, but by and by their objective is to extract as much money from you as possible.

We have a dog named Fred. Fred is a rescue dog that I picked up at our local animal shelter ten years ago, as of this writing, for a nominal fee, in fact, you could say Fred was "free." We love Fred dearly and dread the day he may go to doggy heaven. Yet, Fred has by no means been "free." The first expenditure was one to which I agreed the day I brought him home—he had to be neutered within thirty days or I faced a misdemeanor charge—cha-ching. Then there are all the out of town business trips my wife and I need to take whereby Fred must be boarded—cha-ching, cha-ching. Then Fred developed back problems and he has been on meds for years, two pills he takes daily and a liquid one he takes twice a week—cha-ching, cha-ching. About twice a year, despite all the meds, Fred gets a kink in his back and must be hospitalized for twenty-hours and receive morphine—cha-ching, cha-ching. Then he needs baths and nails trimmed. I figure Fred, a free rescue mutt, has cost at least $5,000 over the years, but we wouldn't give him up for anything.

Your mill is duped into "free" all the time. The worst "free" I can think of is a "free" wire or felt[1]. A clothing supplier wants to break into your mill. They offer you a free or greatly reduced in price clothing substitute for a position on your machine. You'll only be caught by this delusion once—you think, "well we have a change due in that position next week, we'll do it." What is unspoken is the very real danger that this clothing change will negatively affect your productivity or quality, or, even worse, need to be cut off in a time shorter than your normal schedule at the worst time possible—the middle of Saturday night. There is nothing free about this.

I have been a consultant for twenty-five years. Companies are always approaching me about free. My not so nice response is this: I am sorry, I don't need any more opportunities to spread my reputation everywhere. That job is done. Now, why do you think I will be motivated to work for you for free? I am sure if they were good negotiators, they could come up with some logic that might still entice me, but, sadly, I have not seen such cleverness in a long time.

This does not keep companies from thinking that consultants should be free or that they should get a deal from them. I keep mum on the subject, but I will tell you this—if all my clients saw my accounting books, they would be shocked at who is getting a deal (as compared to engaging my competition) and who is

---

[1] For readers not familiar with papermaking, a "wire" or "felt" is an expensive consumable item on a paper machine (often collectively called "clothing") that must be replaced on a regular basis.

not. For again, they all think they are getting a deal. Of course, a consultant offering bad advice which is then blindly followed is no deal at all, even at free—they can be worse than the free clothing.

Let's not end this chapter without easing into the topic of the title of this book (I know, you thought we would never get to it, but you needed background first). This is the personality of consultants. I have always said that as a consultant, you must adopt of stance of being "quietly confident." The consultant that is arrogant you despise and the consultant that is hesitant you don't trust. Hence, the personality of a consultant is paramount. From my side of the table there is more—if I come in and tell you you are doing everything wrong, you will throw me out on my ear; if I tell you are doing everything right, you'll say, "we don't need him." Again, personality is paramount to a successful consulting career—and as a consultant you might actually want to know a few helpful things, too. But—you'll never get to show what you know if you don't have the personality perfected.

Chapter 6—Who loves your mill?

There is an old mill in a coastal southern city for which I haven't bothered to learn the address. I know roughly in which part of town it is located and in the days when I went there, within three blocks of it, I would see evidence of its existence. A recycled mill, it allows (and the poor neighborhood in which it resides tolerates) waste paper to blow all over the neighborhood. Get within three blocks and you can follow the ever-denser waste paper evidence right to the mill door. Do you think anyone on that site, indeed, anyone in its corporate headquarters, loves that mill? Neither do I.

What personalities do you think you will find in such a facility, or perhaps in a visit to their headquarters? I dare say you will find some pretty rough folks with low self-esteem and a bad attitude towards others. My experiences with this facility bear out my perceptions. They are all about making money and taking yours—except they are so blinded by this obsession that I dare say another approach would be far more profitable for them.

Straight north, just about 1,100 miles, is another old mill, perhaps of the same vintage as the first. The owners of this small mill hit the jackpot—a much larger corporation bought them. The old buildings are neat and clean, not just in the front but all the way out the back, too. What I found most amazing though, was the maintenance department. Keep in mind the machines in this mill are open gear, line-shaft driven. This is indeed an old mill. Yet there were tachs and sensors on every motor (except fractional horsepower motors) in the entire place and the electrical maintenance superintendent could sit at his desk and call up each and every motor, tell you its current operating conditions, including its temperature, vibration signature, date installed and projected date to be removed for refurbishment. This was not last week, this was in 2004.

These two mills were not necessarily making the same product, but it would not take much to switch one to the product the other was making. Let's say they were making products in the same broad, general family.

I was there as an adjunct to a team from the new owners who were assessing various aspects of this mill. We were treated graciously (of course, we represented their new owners), but we had a sense they treated everyone this way.

Do you think this mill was loved?

If you are going to understand the personalities of a person, group, or company in this industry, the first question you must ask is this: "Do they love their facility, their company and their industry?"

You don't have to talk to anyone to make this initial assessment—look at the environment they tolerate working in. You will determine if they have high standards or low standards. You will determine if they care for the assets with which they are entrusted. You will essentially be able to tell if they are generally happy or dissatisfied with the place they find themselves in life and in their careers.

And when you determine these qualities, you will be able to predict how they will react to you and how you need to handle them.

This is not an absolute—but a strong indicator: how a person takes care of their surroundings offers many clues as to how they perceive the world, themselves, and others they encounter. This is not the same thing as housekeeping—my office does not meet my highest standards of housekeeping, yet I surround myself there with things about this industry that I love. I am happy in my office. I have been in this same office since 2005, the longest tenure of any office my career. It is me.

People who are happy in their environment reflect that happiness in the way they keep that environment.

I mentioned earlier that the mill I described as being loved was "neat and clean, not just in the front but all the way out the back, too." This is important. Many a mill has a pretty façade. It is going all the way through it and out to the back fence that gives you a real sense of what is going on there.

Many years ago, I was asked to assess a couple of mills in Colombia, in the Cali Valley. I poked around the mills for half a day and then asked to be taken to the water intake, about a half mile away, at the river. It was dangerous country; a small military unit came with us and set up a perimeter with four machine gun nests so that I could examine this operation. When my examination was done, my client asked me why I wanted to go there. I told him if you really want to know how a facility is maintained, or loved, go to the most distance outpost of the operation and see what is going on there. This will tell you nearly everything you need to know. He got a big laugh out of this and heartily agreed. Many people cut the front lawn, but it is how they maintain the back of the mill that shows their true colors. It is a reflection on their willingness to deceive, a strong personality trait you will want to know before dealing with them.

Today, there is a quick way to assess how well a mill is loved. It is not absolute, but it is a preliminary indication and it can give you a preview of what you are headed into before you even leave your home. Best of all, it is free. This great tool is "Google Earth[2]". Pull up Google Earth and zoom in on the facility in question. Look at the roofs of the buildings. If the roofs are in great shape, it is likely the mill is loved. If the roofs are in poor shape, there is even a greater likelihood that no one loves the mill. Why? Roofs protect the assets—if the company is willing to jeopardize the assets by ignoring roof conditions, they are very likely taking other shortcuts, too.

_____

[2] Google Earth is copyright Alphabet Inc. and its affiliated companies.

Section II—Them

Chapter 7—Bullies

Sadly, you did not leave the bullies behind in high school. Now, they have gotten older (note, I did not say they have matured) and reached positions where they can do some real harm, not just break your nose. Unless they have had some counseling or reached an epiphany on their own, they are still bullies.

Being a bully, of course, is a defense mechanism in most cases. Yes, there are sadists who just like to hurt other people for the sake of hurting them, but most bullies are simply scared and insecure little children on the inside.

Bullies are not limited to any unique position or pay grade in your pulp and paper company. They exist at all levels, all corners and all pay grades. Sometimes they cleverly disguise themselves as leaders.

An example is in order.

The CEO of one particular paper company left everyone quaking in their shoes. In the later part of his career, past age fifty, he had honed and polished his game to perfection. For instance, all the leaders of his larger operations were required to fly in to headquarters once a month to report on their operation's performance for the previous month.

This was supposed to be an in and out appearance—from most sites you could fly in the night before and leave the next afternoon. Except if your facility was having a consistently long and difficult struggle meeting its numbers.

These meetings were typically set for 9 o'clock. A reasonable person would take this as 9 a.m.—but not if you were in trouble. In that case, your meeting was going to be at 9 p.m. and you had to find a place to hide on the relatively small senior executive floor in the high rise where headquarters was located. Foolish was the manager who knew they were in trouble and came waltzing in in the middle of the afternoon expecting a 9 p.m. meeting—do that and you missed the meeting because it was then purportedly held at 9 a.m. Of course, if your meeting turned out to be 9 p.m., you had plenty to do—you needed to change your flights, perhaps find a hotel for a second night and so forth.

Think this is enough harassment? Think again, there were other elements to this ritual that affected all who came to bow before the king. His boardroom had had a nice, practical functioning table. He replaced it with a behemoth that nearly filled the room, and except for a mahogany edge of about 4 inches all the way around, its top was beautiful, smooth leather. No one dared open their briefcase on this table for fear of scratching it.

But wait, there's more! This CEO, we'll call him Joey (not his real name) hired 3 or 4 smart as a whip, knock dead gorgeous female MBA's as his assistants. They were called "Joey's Birds" in the whisper conversations in the halls. They sat on either side of him during these inquisitions and spent their time going through your numbers and locating a dollar off here, a penny off there whereupon they would gleefully point out to Joey your incompetence.

There was a funny thing about this whole setup. Joey was never known to fire any one of his direct reports. His system was cleaner and cheaper for the company. If someone was slowly driven nuts by this process, they ran screaming from the building. No severance package, no lawsuits, after all you voluntarily resigned, didn't you?

Bullies deeper in the organization do not behave with such finesse. They are just like they were in elementary or high school, except now they are more powerful because they can ruin your career. I have had the satisfaction of firing a couple of these characters in my four plus decades in the industry—it felt good.

Chapter 8—Clueless

You will find some employees in the backwaters of large corporations who are just simply clueless. They perform some simple mundane tasks efficiently and effectively enough that they are easily kept around for decades to do this. In most cases, computers eventually replace their functions, leaving them out on the street.

Back in the day, I happened to work in a corner of a large engineering department where several disparate functions had been collected. We had a fellow there, bright enough, who had started his career operating a lawn mower for the company. Somehow, I don't think I ever heard the story, he had gotten promoted to an office job.

What was his job? He kept a physical file box full of 3 x 5 cards. Every month he called each pulp and paper mill in the company and asked them the status of certain large spare pieces of equipment. He performed a valuable function—if you had a refiner fail, a very large motor fail or some other such catastrophe, you called him (8 am to 5 pm only please, this was long before cell phones). He could tell you exactly where the spare you needed was located.

Went to lunch with him several times. Nice fellow, personable, friendly. He could no more grasp the scope of the entire company than my dog, Fred. I am sure a bit of software replaced his job long ago.

There used to be many jobs like this; most are gone now.

Chapter 9—Fast Trackers

Fast Trackers come in two types. One reflects the desperation of the large corporation; the other is dangerous. You may be jealous of either one, but that is a mistake—jump ahead and read Chapters 17 and 18 if, upon reflection, the hue coming back from your mirror indicates you are green with envy, it perhaps is justified, perhaps not.

We'll tackle the corporate desperation type first. Large corporations have developed a problem, especially if they are operating in several fields that, while related, are unique in their own ways. So, indulge me a look ahead a bit. The Board of Directors of such a corporation naturally wants a CEO who has a handle on the entire business. Here is where the problem lies.

Again, it is prudent that the CEO understand the entire company. Say this company has fifteen large divisions, not unreasonable these days. To install a CEO who has a couple of years' experience in each of these divisions, you have just chewed up thirty years of their career. Given that some are going to wash out and some are going to be lured by competitors to go elsewhere, the senior management is tasked with finding several mid-twenties-aged promising stars and move them through the system, hoping that in thirty years one outstanding candidate will survive and be ready to take the CEO's job.

It is not easy to be one of these Fast Trackers. I was one once in a company where they were called "Hi-poes", that is "High Potentials." This stood for [identified] High Performance [candidates]. It was a thankless role. Your peers were after you constantly, trying to trip you up.

Several years ago, a money center bank asked me to travel to a mid-south state and look at a mill that their client was thinking of buying and on which the bank wanted my opinion. The place was old, run down and generally decrepit. I remember just one interesting thing from my examination of this facility. At the entrance to the mill manager's office, there was a long list of the people who had occupied that office along with the dates of their tenure. The first name on the list was Sam Smith (not his real name). A legend in the industry, he had been the first mill manager. This was not surprising, for back in the day Mr. Smith had built his reputation starting up mills in the south. What was surprising was another name, about three or four down from Mr. Smith's. This person became a well-known CEO in the industry and has long since retired. If I remember, his tenure at this mill was about eighteen months. Do you think he loved the mill? Refresh yourself with Chapter 6.

This person was the second type of Fast Tracker. He was building his own fast track, and likely you had better not get in his way. Also, don't expect him to spend any more than the bare necessity on maintenance to keep the mill running. He doesn't plan on being there when it comes crashing down due to a lack of maintenance.

This second type of Fast Tracker likes to find a mill that is in pristine condition, then get themselves installed as mill manager. They don't plan on being there long. They cut maintenance, cut staff, cut anything they can. Their objective is to turn in fantastic profit numbers and exit within twenty-four months—just before the maintenance neglect begins to manifest itself.

The poor person that follows them is in for a rough time. They will have to overspend on maintenance in order to maintain status quo. They may have to hire people to fill some of the key jobs (customer service, for instance) that the Fast Tracker cut. They will be lucky to turn a profit in the first couple of years, let alone match their predecessor. All the while, the CEO is beating them up for not doing as well as their predecessor.

Don't be like the second type of Fast Tracker. Not only do they not love their mills, they are cheating the company out of value in the long term to promote themselves. How are they doing this? They are devaluing the physical and human assets through poor maintenance (shortening the life of the physical assets) and failing to build a long-term team (cutting out people who could grow into more responsibility). They are fiduciary frauds.

Chapter 10—Politicians and Opportunists

Politicians and opportunists may, in some cases, or on the surface, seem to be Fast Trackers (already discussed) or Slackers (coming up). They are a bit different.

P & O's, if I may use such an abbreviation, are not particularly interested in going anywhere; they are, however, interested in maximizing benefits accrued to themselves. They will watch the game of "musical offices" and make sure when the time comes they can pounce and get the best digs. The reason they are good at such matters is that they have thought them out weeks, months, or years in advance. While you were dutifully working, they were plotting.

If you have trouble getting straight answers from the human resources department on company benefits for a certain issue, befriend a P & O (keeping in mind they will save the juicy stuff for themselves, but they may throw you a bone to stroke their ego). They have spent time, company time, thoroughly studying every aspect of the company's personnel rules. They know them better than a union president. They know them better than human resources. If the opportunity arises where they can exercise a company rule to their benefit, they will pounce.

P & O's really don't want to go anywhere, because they have invested a great deal of time, albeit time for which the company paid them, learning all the rules where they are. They truly see this as an investment, one they don't want to lose. The best thing a new leader (you) can do, whose mandate is to be a change agent, is move the P & O's around. Move them as far from their comfort zone as befits their skills and abilities and your moving budget. If you can get them into someone else's domain, all the better for you. Most of them will likely quit on you (good thing) but you must carry out a plan that assumes they will not.

Chapter 11—Quiet

This is where the gold is in any organization. The Quiet are the people who chose a profession or avocation, excelled in their studies, acquired a position within a company and just plain do their job every day.

They show up on time, they leave when they are supposed to leave. They are never in the human resources office, either at their initiation or their supervision's initiation.

For all the chest-thumping the leaders do, the Quiet are the glue that keeps the organization running day in and day out.

The best thing a leader can do for these people is make sure the humidity and temperature in their workspace is to their satisfaction and get out of their way as they save your company from all the mistakes you make.

The worst thing a leader can do for these people is try to make them into something they are not. Send them to all the conferences and seminars you can afford on improving their skill sets in their areas of core competency. Never send them to a seminar that is supposed to turn them into a leader. They don't want to be and are ill-suited to be a leader.

If you can, protect them from having to make a presentation to management two or three levels above their position in your company. They will be nervous and look unsure of themselves. Not only have you made them uncomfortable, their poor showing may reflect badly on you.

You see, everyone does not want to be the boss or go on stage. For the Quiet that do their jobs competently day in and day out, this is usually the case.

Be exceedingly happy if you have a company full of the Quiet—they should be two-thirds of your entire employment if you are a decent sized company. Let them earn the profits and cover the mistakes of the other one-third.

Treat them like the gold that they are.

Chapter 12—Slackers

We have all met the Slacker. They may be Bullies. They are not Clueless, Fast Trackers or P & O's. They may look like the Quiet until you dig a bit deeper and find they are unproductive.

Slackers have perfected the art of hiding. Go into any pulp or paper mill of any age and you will find "nests." These are places where Slackers hide out on their shift. Some of them are quite elaborate, equipped with televisions, refrigerators, and game consoles.

Slackers will work harder at not working than if they actually expended the effort to do their job.

We used to say such people exhibited sociopathic behavior. The DSM (See Prelude) today characterizes this as "antisocial personality disorder." Simply, they don't want to play the game as defined by civilized society and business (More on this in Chapter 13—Slackers are not the only ones afflicted with this disorder).

These employees must be rooted out and terminated. They are a drain on the company. As a caution, however, they may not go quietly. Depending on the depth of their "antisocial personality disorder" these may be the ones to return to your facility with guns and a grudge.

It is a poor reflection on management when a deep tour of a facility is taken and nests are found. This is an indication of a superficial attitude towards one's responsibilities as a manager.

Having said this, however, let me hasten to say, all Slackers are not in the hourly ranks. There are plenty in management ranks or otherwise occupying an office.

This implies that becoming a Slacker can be an acquired attribute and this is true. Denied a promotion or recognition, someone may slip into this behavior as an expression of their own cynicism and rebellion.

One of the best examples of a Slacker I ever witnessed was a person in an engineering department in a mill who got in the habit of being picked up by one of the resident contractors every morning about 9:30 am and going to a local restaurant for a piece of pie and coffee. We called this activity "pie time."

I have not provided a separate chapter for crooks, for most of the time, crooks are a subset of Slackers. Slackers just steal time from the company; crooks take it a step further and steal resources.

In my Nip Impressions weekly column, I highlight crooks each August with a series called "Pulp Rats." These are stories that have become known about employees and others who outright steal from their employers.

Chapter 13—Board Members

I have had the misfortune of being on the board of a small publicly traded company. I was once interviewed (and failed the interview) to be on the board of a moderate sized company in our industry. Off and on, I have been a member of NACD—the National Association of Corporate Directors. I have been on more volunteer boards than I care to name.

We have a family friend who, having served as the controller of a major international company, one with some of the most well recognized brands in the world, is in high demand to serve on smaller boards in her retirement—as the head of the audit committee.

So, this is the short version of the composition of Boards of Directors. Most members (except maybe those who head audit or regulatory subcommittees which have real work to do) seem to me to be there for the perks, at least from their point of view. From the CEO's point of view, or perhaps the Chair's point of view, they are there to support the Chair or CEO. Dissent is often not wanted or expected. There is a huge argument going on at Tesla at this time about this very matter. It has occurred since Tesla's market value has exceeded General Motors. It is contended by some traders that the board is packed with the CEO's friends (who have been given big stock options).

I like to think we have better boards than this in the pulp and paper industry, but an examination of board actions over the last 15 or twenty year may not be encouraging. If you are a board member or close to a board in our industry, I hope your experience is better than mine.

Want to know if a board is effective and on top of their game? Don't look at their earnings performance, which will be in line with their peers. A good place to look is at the safety record of their company. If they don't have an ever-improving safety record, I would suggest there is an underlying desperation for profits or a callous view of their most important asset—their employees. Both, taken together or separately, speaks volumes about the board's performance.

There is yet another way to look at board performance which I already mentioned in Chapter 6. See the last part of that chapter and my discussion there on roof conditions.

It is really quite simple—the safety record indicates the board's attitude towards protecting their most valuable assets—employees. The roof conditions indicate their attitude towards protecting their second most valuable assets—the equipment and processes used to store raw materials, manufacture products and store finished goods. With a bit of research, you can assess their seriousness in maintaining both these fiduciary duties before you ever step onto the property. Earnings achieved by the neglect of these two are "cheap earnings."

In the case where a Wall Street activist has decided the company is undervalued and needs drastic surgery, all I just said is invalid. If this activist can successfully gather enough voting shares to elect one or two board members of their own, all hell will break loose, because their objective is to bring about drastic change. The board will be thrown in disarray because the legacy members are used to rubber stamping the Chair's wishes. Now what to do? Whose resolutions to vote for?

Remember Ross Perot? He didn't understand this anymore than I did. He sold his software company, EDS, to one of, at the time, most ossified corporations in America—General Motors.

As part of the deal, they made him a board member. Big mistake. He thought he was supposed to contribute something as a board member. After several months of angst, they paid him another boatload of money to resign from the board. Our industry is better than it used to be, but you can rest assured there are still plenty of pulp and paper companies' boards of directors that need to be shaken and stirred.

This is not to say all activists are great, either. Robert Maxwell tore through the U.K. publishing business in the 1980's. He was definitely an activist. I am not so sure he did the industry much good. If I remember, it was alleged he committed suicide by drowning off one of his yachts. Likely he should have read Chapter 20 of this book.

Section III—Best fit

In truth, a simple one machine mill only needs one person who has a degree from what is known as a "pulp and paper school." With the title of production manager or machine superintendent, this person had better have around twenty years' experience. I am not saying more employees with such educations is not better, I am describing the minimalist condition.

I have spent a lot of time observing and thinking about whether the top executive on a site should possess pulp and paper education credentials. My conclusion is perhaps a wide, expansive view of the industry and the particular company for which they work, coupled with an understanding of modern finance and accounting may be a better choice. My caution is they must be knowledgeable enough of the technical aspects of the company's business to avoid stupid, physics-defying decisions. They also need to understand the scale of routine expenditures in a mill and not starve it for necessary cash, particularly for maintenance. Beyond that, they should have plenty of support beneath them (which they trust and heed) to handle the strategic and tactical technical decisions.

The most important positions for a company are in sales. For without sales, you cannot spin the invoice printer and you cannot stay in business. When I was a young engineer, I looked down on sales, thinking they did not have my education—that was a stupid analysis. We must have competent sales people.

Of course, sales people come in all levels of competence, just like they do in any other aspect of business. I happen to think the best ones come out of medical sales, particularly medical device sales. They have been trained to do one-on-one sales and they have been used to getting their price. They are not the typical order taker sales person who was common in the pulp and paper industry when I was younger.

There has been a trend to move towards more technically competent sales people over the years. Product specifications have become more exacting and measurable, and on the customer end, the purchasers and their assistants have used this to improve the quality coming in the door. The days of the golfing, glad-handing sales person are long over.

Supplier companies often like to hire senior folks from production companies as senior level sales people. Many times, this does not turn out to be a good fit. Those recently leaving the producer companies are shocked about how deferential they must behave towards the customers and contacts as they become supplier sales people. They dislike all the travel. Then, from the supplier side, there is often the shock of how small is the universe of contacts the production people really know. Most of these relationships do not last more than a few years.

The technical department should be operated at least by well-grounded scientists, and this is another place that is a great opportunity to make these scientists pulp and paper graduates, although a good chemist can do fine in this position. But given all other attributes, what is the strongest one needed in this department? Honesty.

True story from long ago. I took over the auxiliary services in a mill, including the technical department. This was long before any computers had been introduced to this area of the mill. I asked for an orientation tour of the department. On this tour, I was shown three four-drawer file cabinets. These contained the papers recording tests from the products made in the mill. In every case, there were three sheets of paper stapled together. The administrative assistant glibly showed me that the back page was the original tests, the middle page was a copy of the back page, marked up by the technical department manager, and the top page was a copy of the one she typed and sent to the customer, based on the middle page. Everything was fiction! To the department manager's credit, if he deserved any, upper management had refused to repair the HVAC system in the department so that it could maintain TAPPI[3] standard conditions of humidity and temperature. So, in essence, it was all fiction, and gladly now, all the people involved in this charade were gone from this site. We fixed the equipment and started reported tests honestly.

To me it has seemed the best leadership has always come from the military. After all, if you can persuade someone to go out in the field and take a bullet, persuading them to do their job in a pulp or paper mill should be simple. Yet I have seen some problems with junior military officers, the academy graduates recently eligible for returning to civilian life. The problem here is they often see the standards of discipline and expectations in pulp and paper mills to be so low compared to their experience in the military that assimilating is very, very hard for them. They have also discovered they have lost the tools for discipline the military provides. Hence, I suspect they see the entire pool of employees in a pulp and paper facility as one large bowl of Jell-O. Work with them to align their expectations for themselves and their employees with the civilian world and things will work out (unless they have a pushy spouse at home who thinks they should be getting a promotion twice a year). I like high level

---

[3] Technical Association of the Pulp and Paper Industry

non-commissioned officers from the Sargent ranks. They know how to get things done and are promotable.

Where do you find the best maintenance people, management, or hourly ranks? Hire out of the hospitals. Hospital maintenance personnel, especially if they had any responsibility for maintaining surgical rooms, are the best. They are better than airplane mechanics. First, the equipment they are used to working on is more nearly like that in paper mills. In hospitals, they are closer to the beneficiaries of their work, the patients, than are airplane mechanics. For airplane mechanics, the passengers can be a bit of an abstract.

Is there any place for the tough and the stubborn? Sometimes. I needed to change out the superintendent in a powerhouse once. The person in the job was not a leader and was being pushed around by the hourly workers and their shop steward. I looked at my group of maintenance foremen and found one who was honest, tough, and stubborn. Promoted him to powerhouse superintendent. Problem solved.

The worst credibility issue to be encountered in an older mill is when the top level of management rotates through about every two years, and, further, they live fifty miles away in a nice little white picket fence town. Management should live within a thirty-minute drive to the mill. No exceptions. They need to be there to deal with 24/7 issues and they need to leave an image with the hourly folks that they are not too good for them, they can live in their communities. Some argue that the mill manager's kid should not be in little league where the night shift superintendent is the umpire, and I get that. But this is an opportunity to put everyone on an equal basis and the opportunity should not be lost.

Back when "trimming out" the machine was a largely manual task, mathematicians were the best selection for this role, for it is a simple math job. I would still hire mathematicians for this job, because I want someone who understands how the programs work.

One of our biggest problems in many areas of the mill today is we have people operating computers that know very little about the math and science behind the computer screen so they are forced to believe it is true whether it is or not. In nearly all cases, it pays to hire employees with a practical viewpoint.

Section IV—You

Chapter 14—Goals

You have had goals and there are hundreds of books written on career goal setting. So, you might be asking, "Jim, why are you wasting your time on this?"

All I ask you to do is read this book up to this Chapter, jump ahead and read Chapters 17 – 19, read Section V, and finally read The Final Chapter. Then, come back here and write down your (perhaps) modified goals after you have had a chance to think about them (a couple of days).

Your next question I have already anticipated is this: "Jim, if you wanted me to read the book in that order, why was it not presented in that order?" Answer: this book was carefully designed with a certain symmetry. To present it in any other form would violate that symmetry—it is you, dear reader, who is unsymmetrical and needs a wee bit of adjusting.

An important consideration most people miss is that every day they should be working on their resume or curriculum vitae through the tasks they are doing. If you are doing tasks that you would not put on your resume, may I ask why? Sure, your boss is going to ask you to do things off track occasionally and they may take a week or two. But if they take longer than that, you have a serious problem. You are getting off goal. Time to talk to your mentor or psychologist about what is going on. It may make perfectly good sense and is truly an opportunity that merits changing course, but it must be a stop and evaluate experience.

Indulge me on goals and the circuitous reading path.

Thanks.

The next chapter is where we get into goals in detail.

Chapter 15—All great leaders are actors

I have never known a great leader who was not a great actor. Go back and watch the fantastic movie "Patton" starring George C. Scott. It is nearly fifty years old, but it clearly demonstrates when Patton was acting in front of his troops to inspire them and, in private, when Patton's real emotions showed up.

The difference for you is—there is no place for you to let your real self show unless you fully follow my advice in Section V. A mistake of a place to vent your frustrations as a leader is at home with your family. All this does for you is sour relations with your spouse and your children—it solves nothing. Give them the highlights of the positives, an occasional negative in order for them to understand you don't work in an ideal world, and that's it. If they ask, share, be circumspect and don't give away any company secrets.

A friend of mine is the CEO of a major box manufacturing company. His family lives well, appropriate for their station in life. His kids have always understood this. When one of his sons got old enough to ask, his dinner table question was, "Dad, what does your company do?" Response: "Make empty boxes." It didn't take a minute for the son to decide this was a perilous path and the lifestyle to which he had become accustomed must be at risk. It took a bit of explaining to get the child back to a level of comfort. This is OK—introduce realism.

Being an actor is much harder than letting it all hang out, so to speak, but far more effective. In some situations, being an actor is the only way to accomplish the goals you have set for your area of responsibility and for yourself (don't forget—there will be a Final Chapter event here).

So, make a list, looking out for yourself first:

1. How do I expect my resume (curriculum vitae) to look when I reach the Final Chapter of this assignment? What accomplishments will I be able to highlight?
2. How will my area of responsibility look when I reach the Final Chapter? What will be...
   a. the safety record?
   b. the profitability?
   c. the market share?
   d. the employment?
   e. the net assets employed (undepreciated investment)?

Now, what will be my act and posture as relates to

1. My boss and other superiors?
2. My peers?
3. My subordinates?
4. Customers?
5. Suppliers?

Each one of these will take much thought and will need a written outline from you. The good news is this: by and large, you can start on this right now, even if you are still in school—it makes no difference who the people are. You are not writing this for individuals, you are writing it for the roles they fulfill. Certainly, once you meet these people you can tweak things slightly to match with their personalities, but you really need to do the hard work only once and simply modify based on your experience and plan in the next act. I have seen very successful managers who obviously had done this and repeated (with tweaks as they gained experience) the same playbook as they moved from assignment to assignment.

Way back in Chapter 3, we talked about Jeff Bezos and Bill Gates. Don't you think, even in their early years, they had a plan developed something like I have outlined above, ready to immediately put in place when the correct opportunity presented itself? I do. You can too, and you are never too old to start.

It is understood, you keep all this private, very private. Expect to only "let your hair down" with two or three industry associates in your entire career. This is a team sport, but not in the normal sense. If you aspire to be the leader, it is a lonely road.

Above we talked about the how. The next question is how long do you have to put your changes in place? The old conventional wisdom was you had a year: "After a year, you own it." My feeling is this has been compressed to nine months. You still need about three months on the front end to assess what you have inherited. This gives you only six months to put your plan in place.

Here is as good a place as any to talk about your failures, for you will have failures. When you are receiving a "dressing down" by your boss, accept it fully and respectfully. Ask questions at the end if you need clarification. Never offer excuses or explanations, especially early in the conversation, preferably never. Never be defensive. To do so will make you look like an amateur, nervous, and—defensive. These postures will not help your case or your reputation.

In your act, you will want to have an opportunity to blow up occasionally. Keeps people on their toes. I had a chance to watch my mentor up close for several years. At the time, his "blow ups" seemed to be entirely random. I thought about this for many years and finally confronted him. "Your 'blow ups' were completely random, weren't they?"

"Yes. You see when you make your 'blow ups' about a specific topic, then your subordinates never bring that topic up again. They hide it from you. When your 'blow ups' are infrequent but completely random, they are on their toes all the time but continue to bring you all their problems. They have no idea what causes you to go berserk."

A word of caution. I am talking about leaders and subordinates that were born long before the current millenniums. We know from the popular press that millenniums are generally not ready for the rigors of the work force. It will take some special preparation to get them ready. Yet, it must be done if your company is to survive and thrive. Sadly, it is beyond my expertise.

Chapter 16—All great leaders have flaws

General David Petraeus looked like the perfect military leader until he got caught handing classified materials to his (female) biographer. More on this particular flaw in Chapter 17.

Morgan, Rockefeller, Carnegie, and Ford were all great leaders with flaws. Carnegie attempted to assuage his perceived guilt as to how he had operated his businesses (the fatal Homestead Mill strike; the Johnstown Flood), once he had an epiphany, by building a library in every tiny town in America and a great music hall in New York.

People driven to roles of leadership tend to be sociopathic. We discussed this back in Chapter 12 when we were talking about slackers. I also revealed that the DSM today prefers "antisocial personality disorder." If you think about many leaders you have known or have read about, you'll see where they often have a touch of this.

Besides leadership and slacking, sociopathic behavior is also associated with the criminal mind. No better example of this exists today than Bernie Madoff, ensconced in the Federal Prison in Butner, North Carolina. As I understand it, the other inmates there treat Mr. Madoff with great respect, for they see that he succeeded beyond their wildest dreams in fleecing John Q. Public. He is a hero to them.

In the Far East to this day, leaders found flawed tend to commit suicide. The loss of face in the Japanese culture, for instance, is so great they cannot face even their families. Perhaps we need more such contriteness here (however, I am not advocating suicide!).

I have been up close and personal to enough high level Wall Street meetings to see at least one aspect of how things can go wrong. The scenario is this—we have an owner/developer in the room very much wanting to do a certain deal. I am there vouching for the cost estimate. The lenders are there. The equity players are there. Perhaps there is a development authority that is throwing in some cash, too, if certain covenants are made (these are usually based on how many construction and permanent jobs will be created). When all the pieces are fit together, there is tremendous pressure put on all involved to make it happen. Did I mention there are a raft of lawyers there, too? —there are so many of them you cannot keep track of who is working for what party, let alone whether any of them are looking out for doing what is legal, let alone moral and ethical.

Such meetings can go on for several long days. You can imagine how intense the pressure becomes to find a weak spot to exploit and save the day. Fortunately, I can say in over twenty-five years' participation in these exercises, I can say I have never seen one go over the legal edge—but I am not a lawyer.

But you can see how they can. In the news, you have seen the results.

Point to ponder—How many seriously flawed leaders "love the mill? (Chapter 6)."

Chapter 17—The role of cussing and finesse

I grew up in a home where the word "darn" was not uttered, let alone, "pee" or "butt." The words "God" or "Jesus" were not used except in reverential deity reference. I recognize that there has been a sea-change in what is acceptable language in my lifetime, but I still think language, and the perceived strength of it, has a valuable role to play in leadership.

So does its delivery—I have a longtime friend who loathes delivering messages in writing (notes, email, or letters—he calls this "murder by memo") but won't hesitate to tell you what he thinks to your face, often with great finesse.

However, if you must use email, our youngest daughter has perfected a method that will most likely keep you out of trouble. She inserts the subject of the email next to last and the name of the recipient last. In this way, she says you have no chance of sending off an email that is half completed and a better chance of cooling down from the likelihood of sending an email that should never be sent to start with. Excellent advice.

If my mother could have heard the language I used by the time I was a twenty something working in industry, I would have been completely embarrassed and died of shame. I am not proud of what I can only describe as an insecure weakling's substitute for confidence. When I hear someone cussing a lot, I think they are not a very deep thinker, and are rude or inarticulate. Not adjectives with which one wants to be associated.

To this day, I don't invoke any of the deity's names separately or with the word "damn." I can count on one hand the two or three times I have let this slip in my life.

As for the rest of the cussing repertoire, sometimes it is critical you get people's attention by startling them and cussing is a good way to do it. At the same time, you can't startle them if they are used to hearing you say those words on a regular basis.

Look at the world of comedy. Comedians are always desperate for audience recognition. When they run out of funny, original material, they resort to raunchy stories and what used to be called filthy language. But it has ceased to work; they have inoculated the audiences and created an expectation that this is what you will hear. Clean comics have been making a limited inroad in recent years because audiences are worn out on the bad language routine.

In work, the same thing can happen. Hopefully, I have cleaned up my language enough that this following scenario would have an effect, for it would be startling to the listener. A framing member is being placed in a paper machine. For some reason, it has slipped and appears to be about to tip over on Jeff, who is looking the other direction. I can't get to Jeff, but I can yell "Jeff, get the f--- out of the way." Hopefully Jeff has been conditioned to my voice, startled by what I said, and has time to react and run because he perceives it is serious. Would I hesitate to use this approach because I perceive my saintly Mother is flapping her angelic wings over my shoulders? Not for a second—it just might save Jeff's life. I'll gladly take the beating from Mother later.

———

Finesse is the other side of the speech coin.

In some of my other writings, I have mentioned the horrible ways I have seen sales people treat customers. For goodness sakes, customers are the only way you can spin your invoice printer. You don't want to let them run over you (there *is* a time to walk away from a customer when they have just gotten too expensive to keep), but most of the time you want to err on the side of making sure their every legal, moral, and ethical need has been met.

One of the greatest mistakes I have seen with customers is that sales assumes that customers are our friends. Customers are never our friends in the traditional sense of the word. What we want to make sure is they are never our enemies. For years, I have told my own sales people that the customer relationship is like dating and should proceed at that pace (or at least the pace we were familiar with in the 1970's—from what I read now, dating has the finesse of turning a bull loose in a pasture full of yearlings).

Of course, finesse works with employees, too. I just felt customers were more important to first mention in order to aid you in keeping your invoice printer spinning.

Finesse with employees, if not faked (and they can spot fake a mile away), should be designed to improve productivity, then morale.

Finesse can include scaring employees to death (they are going to lose their job or be demoted), but this has a short fuse. Humans can only tolerate being scared for a finite period. After that they act and find a way to move to a less threatening environment, even if to a poorer paying, poorer benefits position.

You may not consider this finesse, but it is a story I recall from *Forbes Magazine* several years ago. It involves the Quick Trip, or QT, convenience store and gas station chain, which is based in Oklahoma. They happen to be here in Atlanta as well, where I live, and I think they are great. All stores are absolutely spit-polish clean inside and out, day and night. How can they be so reliably clean and of high quality? According to the *Forbes* story, when the CEO was new and not well known, he was doing his own "secret shopper" inspections of the stores. He came upon a store that was not up to standard. What did he do? Within a week that store was bulldozed, employees fired and freshly planted grass seed was in its place. That is finesse.

Normally, I say praise in public and discipline in private, but this CEO of this large chain should be commended for finding the most economical way to send an important message to the entire corporation. Can you think of a faster way to send a message to all your employees? I'll bet he didn't even have to write an email or letter.

A bit more about morale—don't set your standards so high no one can reach them. At least 5% of your employees should be able to attain the highest bar you set. How you reward them and publicize their reward is finesse. Hint, they must be employees that the rank and file largely agree are the best in the company for their given rank and pay grade—that requires the leader to know his people and be assured he is awarding the deserving, not the popular.

But Jim, *what is finesse?* My thinking on this, if pressed, is fully grasping the scope and scale of a problem, formulating an answer that leaves all parties involved at the highest state of morale possible, yet achieves the objectives required by the entity that employs you.

You may wish to remember this another way—TKN. Don't say something to an employee unless it is the Truth, Kind and Necessary. That is finesse.

Chapter 18—Dangers beyond age 40

You may have heard it said teenagers are hormones with legs. In other words, teenagers think they are thinking with their brains, but particularly when it comes to love interests, the hormones are doing the thinking. They are being deceived into thinking their brains are doing all the work.

I have some sad news for you. For many, after a sabbatical of ten to twenty years, the hormones take over again. Only this time we really know we are thinking with our brains, don't we, so everything we are doing is rational, isn't it? Ha!

If you are a male executive, go buy yourself a Corvette—it is cheaper, and we are just talking financially, than what you are contemplating doing. If you are a female executive and the chief breadwinner in your house, may I suggest a Tesla for the same reason?

It is not unheard of today for midlevel managers in their early fifties to be dividing assets and paying alimony approaching at least $10,000 per month (plus the other side's lawyer fees and all court costs).

Get yourself counseling, work it out—and not just for the money.

Reaching forty, there are other problems beyond the obvious one of wandering lust (or hopelessness in one's current situation) which I alluded to above. The most obvious one is the manager who, experiencing twenty years of success, suddenly thinks they are infallible and irreplaceable.

These problems manifest themselves in many ways. It could be the manager starts making completely crazy decisions. After all, they know it all now.

More likely, they will decide they need to shakedown the company (privately) or suppliers (not quite so privately) for more money. After all, they argue in their own mind, they are just not being paid for all the great work they are doing for the company. Most get caught, but some do not (I know of a few cases like this but the statute of limitations has long since run out).

If they are satisfied with small change, they cheat on expense reports. Notice: cheating on expense reports for ten years can add up and get you a sentence of the Bernie Madoff class.

The prisons contain many people who were caught up in their own hubris and thought they had learned how to beat the system. This is a dead-end track.

Simply, in our forties and fifties, we can think we are invincible, and, foolishly, act accordingly. We are not.

Chapter 19—Centering yourself

Since about the mid-1920's (with the advent of radio), civilizations have unknowingly measured their worth through the messages advertisers have told us. Think about all the things you think you need or want that have been delivered to you via retail advertisement. You can't, because advertising is an integral part of our everyday lives. Confession, I make my living with Business-to-Business advertising, but I rationalize this by saying to myself the purchasing decisions in this area are made with a cost benefit analysis (most of the time).

What I am talking about now is retail advertising, advertising that persuades you that you need a new car, home, watch or clothes. A different credit card. All things bought without much thought or analysis, just because we think we "need" them. (Confession: as of this writing, we have three *Amazon Alexa Echoes* in our home—one on each floor). Sometimes this is called "keeping up with the Joneses." Therefore, we need centering activities that are outside this realm. Commercial advertising, while valuable in some ways, can end up destructively consuming us in others. Constantly buying the latest this or thinking we need the latest that consumes current income and drastically affects long term retirement income. Additionally, the satisfaction from a purchase is extremely short-lived. The whole process becomes a frantic never-ending cycle ruining our health, our employment, and our relationship with other people. It is a dead-end road.

I am a Christian. Raised in a Christian home, been a Christ follower since I understood what this means. Since this is a secular book, I leave it at that but included it because it is the first activity in my effort to center myself when work, which I dearly love, gets too crazy.

It is important to have some centering activities that allow you to take work out of your mind for your mind needs a rest from work.

For seven years, I was in the Georgia State Defense Force which is an all-volunteer adjunct to the Georgia National Guard. I can tell you, when you have a training weekend, all matters about work will leave your mind.

Since 2011, Laura and I have gone to Guatemala approximately seven times each to work with *Porch de Salomon (Porchedsalomon.org)*. Helps us get away and is quite humbling. Laura loves to work with the mothers and children, I like to work on construction. I took a team of papermakers there in 2016 and plan on doing this again very soon. No thinking about work there.

Laura and I have taken ballroom dancing lessons for the last couple of years. No thinking about work there.

We like to go on cruises—a complete escape.

I like to do solo long-distance automobile drives. Actually, I like to have Fred along. Last count, he has been in twenty-three states.

An economical way to clear your mind is to go camping and don't be a wimp—force yourself to cook all the meals at the campsite. This will clear your mind for the weekend. You will learn how hard it is to keep from going hungry when you lose the modern conveniences and restaurants.

A friend of mine takes many online graduate level courses. No degree objective here, he just likes to learn about nearly everything.

Others own boats, hike, run marathons, you name it. You must have an avocation that is effective at turning off your mind to work.

The opposite and dark side of this. I knew a young engineer who was at the right time and place to become involved in process modeling for pulp and paper mills. He got good at it, started his own business. Hired people, bought an airplane.

When I first met this man, he was a skinny mid-twenties engineer working for a major pulp and paper company. The last time I saw him, after his "success", we went to dinner. He was morbidly obese, he ordered three or four hard drinks before dinner and wine with dinner. The situation was so out of control I made a casual comment.

Within two years, one evening he dropped dead at this desk from a heart attack.

You must get away from your work, and I am looking in a mirror as I say this. I have been doing better in my latter years, should have started much earlier.

Find something that forces your mind to not think about work for a at least a weekend or two a month. Your brain needs the rest.

Chapter 20—More money will not make you happier

I see young engineers in this industry who own luxury cars, live in the finest homes and are in debt up to their eyeballs.

I have met older members of our industry who confess to having bought too many cars when they were young, and although they would like to retire, can't because of their indiscretions in their early days.

I bought too many cars in my early days. Fortunately, my wife has done an excellent job of planning for our retirement so my only excuse for working is that I love this industry and can't get it out of my system. We are not rich, but we will make it. I can't imagine not having something to do with the pulp and paper industry, so retirement in the usual sense does not appeal to me.

There are four pieces of advice I have for you when it comes to your paycheck. These apply at any age. Start with the next one you receive.

1. Find charitable organizations you are interested in supporting and faithfully give them at least 10% of the gross each month. This will humble you.
2. Save 10% of the gross each month in solid retirement investments.
3. Live on the rest with the goal of doing this on a cash basis (except for perhaps a home mortgage) within five years. Can't do this? Think about it—you will still be living better than 99% of the world.
4. Tip your hotel maid. At least $20, often $40. Don't take it out of the 10% mentioned above and don't record it

on your expense report. Take it out of your pocket. It is just the right thing to do.

Dave Ramsey says it best: "We borrow money we don't have to buy things we don't want to impress people we don't like." Dave Ramsey is no flake and if you have not taken his course, I suggest you find one and sign up for it (and no, I am not a paid endorser, I just happen to believe in this).

But this is a book about "Personalities in the Pulp and Paper Industry." Just imagine how much better your personality will become if you are not putting pressure on yourself to get the next promotion next week just because you think the money will solve your problems.

Follow the above advice and you might just be able to calmly practice your profession. You might concentrate on the short courses furnished by your company to learn the materials rather the spending all the time in the course scheming and conniving how it will get you ahead.

This change in the way you live will bring you more peace, help your personality improve, perhaps more than anything else in this book, and is the path to get you ahead in your job because you will start thinking rationally again.

I once worked for a boss who was delighted when any employee (that he wanted to keep) bought a fancy new car or house. His logic "now I've got 'em."

Is that the way you want to live?

Section V—So now what? Tests, Mentors, Psychological Counseling, and taking care of your health

A friend of mine who has been a very successful CEO in our industry and is now retired, does not like to use testing when hiring employees. He is a very skilled interviewer (in Vietnam he was taught Vietnamese and was prized as an interrogator). His reasoning? Testing makes the workforce too homogeneous and he would rather build unique perspectives throughout the company—he thinks it makes the company stronger, sort of like having a mutt (Fred) instead of an AKC purebred.

I prefer testing; I am not that great of an interrogator. I also like to take them myself. There are many tests available, from skills to psychological. I'll not mention one by name except the Predictive Index (or PI). It has been around since the mid-1950's and been given thousands of times. Taking the test is so simple and to some so ridiculous that their attitude just taking the test can somewhat affect the outcome. However, skilled interpreters can even detect this. I have included the most recent results for myself at the end of this section.

Be comfortable enough and curious enough with yourself to take solid, legitimate industrial psychology tests. It will improve your performance and make you more valuable to your employer.

You also need a mentor, two if possible. I have been fortunate enough to have had a great mentor for most of my career. Bright and articulate, he has kept me centered when I was headed off the rails. But don't just go grab a mentor—finding one of quality is far more important than speed here.

How do you find a mentor of quality? Look at their record of accomplishment. Look how they got through their forties (see Chapter 18). Make sure they possess a broad scope. Some highly successful people are an inch wide and three miles deep. This won't help you—it is extremely unlikely you will be in exactly the same niche. Settle for one two miles deep and two miles wide. Good mentors spend more time talking about you than talking about themselves, too. They are genuinely interested in what you are doing and will give it to you straight when you are messing up. Don't expect every conversation to be friendly and reinforcing in reference to what you have been doing—after all you can get unlimited affection from a dog.

Then, the last item you need in your tool kit is a psychologist and, if necessary, a reference to a psychiatrist.

I have been going to a psychologist since around 2003. I skipped a couple of years but then decided (actually, my wife decided!) I needed to go back to him. So, once a month, my calendar is cleared and he and I sit and talk about me. He is great and has done his homework. Call this extreme mentoring.

And Laura and I go one step further. We have been going to a marriage counselor for 19 years of our 20-year marriage. We are both previously married and we are committed that this is our last marriage. Thus, we block out an hour a month and make a visit to our counselor. Well worth the time and money.

Professionals not in your family can help far more than "free" in cost and time to keep you on a healthy track. I urge you to overcome any personal biases against these services and discover what they can do for you.

Laura even has me going to a pedicurist and masseuse. This helps my attitude of wellbeing, too.

Then there is your general health. This is an asset in which your employer has a large investment. Simply, the longer you stay, the more you learn, the more responsibility you are given, the more valuable you are.

Your short-term illnesses, your long-term illnesses, your chronic illnesses, and your psychological health are important to your employer. These matters are just as important to your employer as the physical assets and other human resources they place under your control. Yet, repeatedly, I see people try to play "superman" when it comes to their own health. People who are very conscientious when it comes to other assets put under their control, have some sort of blockage when it comes to managing these assets most important to themselves and their employer.

Perhaps it is because I am a three-time cancer survivor, but I must say I am very in tune with what my body is telling me, for I know if I don't notice the signals, I am dead.

I wish more people would be this way, for the sake of themselves and their employer.

Men are particularly bad about ignoring the signs of a heart attack. If you study this subject, you'll learn you have at least a one week warning, often much longer. A heart attack is nothing like what you might have seen portrayed in the media.

Chronic coughs mean something serious is wrong. If you are coughing for more than two weeks, you have a problem that needs a doctor's attention.

Psychological problems, particularly those caused by internally generated chemical imbalances, are another. If you think the world is out of balance, you just might want to seek professional help to make sure the problem isn't internal. These issues can be very tricky and need to be dealt with quickly—I speak from experience in my own immediate family.

In short, this body we have is a miracle, but it is frail. As it gets older, it acquires diseases and is not as resilient as it was when it was younger. Pay attention to it, listen to what it is telling you, for the sake of yourself and your employer. It is an asset in which both you and your employer have a great deal of interest.

Jim Thompson
Survey Date : 10/2/2014
Report Date : 10/2/2014

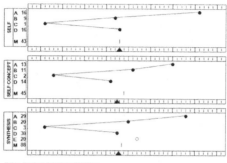

PI for: Jim Thompson Date: 10/2/2014
Copyright © 1994-2000, 2002, 2005 by Praendex, Inc. All rights reserved.

The results of the Predictive Index® survey should always be reviewed by a trained Predictive Index analyst. The PI® report provides you with a brief overview of the results of the Predictive Index® and prompts you to consider many aspects of the results not contained in the overview. If you have not yet attended the Predictive Index Management Workshop™, please consult someone who has attended in order to complete the report.

STRONGEST BEHAVIORS

Jim's PI Pattern is extremely wide, which means that his behaviors are very strongly expressed and his needs are very strongly felt.

Jim will most strongly express the following behaviors:

- Intense proactivity and aggressiveness in driving to reach his goals. Actively and boldly challenges the world, his business, and even others' areas within his business.

- Strongly independent in putting forth his own ideas, which are innovative and original, and if implemented, will change the organization. Resourceful and forceful in overcoming obstacles, he vigorously and directly attacks problems; fights back hard when challenged.

- Incredibly strong sense of urgency; he's in nearly constant motion, putting pressure on himself and others for immediate results. Unable to do routine work.

- Task-focused; he quickly notices and pushes to fix technical problems, assertively cutting through any personal/emotional issues. Has aptitude to spot trends in data or figure out how complex systems work.

79

- Independent, analytical, critical, and creative thinking and action; little need for external validation before action. Private.

- Authoritative and direct, he's driven to accomplish his personal goals; he pushes through roadblocks assertively. Communication is direct, to the point, and sometimes brusque.

SUMMARY

Jim is an intense, results-oriented, self-starter whose drive and sense of urgency are tempered and disciplined by his concern for the accuracy and quality of his work. His approach to anything he does or is responsible for will be carefully thought-out, based on thorough analysis and detailed knowledge of all pertinent facts.

Strongly technically-oriented, he has confidence in his professional knowledge and ability to get things done quickly and correctly. With experience, he will develop a high level of expertise in his work and will be very aware of mistakes made either by himself or anybody doing work under his supervision. Jim takes his work and responsibilities very seriously and expects others to do the same.

In social matters, Jim is reserved and private, with little interest in small talk. His interest and his energy will be focused primarily on his work, and in general he is more comfortable and open in the work environment than he is in purely social situations. In expressing himself in his work environment he is factual, direct, and authoritative.

Imaginative and venturesome, Jim is a creative person, capable of developing new ideas, systems, plans or technology, or of analyzing and improving old ones. He relies primarily on his own knowledge and thinking, with little reference to others, to get things done. He sets a high, exacting standard for himself, and generally finds that others do not meet that standard. To earn his trust, someone must consistently meet that standard and get results; if they can do that, Jim will do whatever he can to work with them whenever he needs to collaborate.

While he may be perceived by other people as aloof, he will earn their respect for his knowledge of his work and the soundness of his decisions.

MANAGEMENT STYLE

As a manager of people or projects, Jim will be:

- Both broadly focused and tactically cognizant; strategic thinking is the first priority moderated by a drive for details, accuracy, and correctness

- Self-reliant and independent with a great deal of confidence in his ideas, opinions, and knowledge; he'll have definite opinions about how things should be done and prefers at least some hands-on knowledge of what he manages

- Hesitant to delegate authority or details; his follow-up is close and critical ensuring that his team has completed all work to his exacting standards

- Fast paced and eager for results, tempered by a drive to ensure accuracy and completeness; he interprets deadlines literally and drives his team hard to meet them

- Slow to trust others until they have produced accurate, timely results consistently

- Demanding, creative, and exacting; always striving to do things better, faster, and with greater precision; he focuses more on solving problems than celebrating or praising solutions

INFLUENCING STYLE

As an influencer, Jim will be:

- Authoritative and assertive in influencing others towards his goal
- Driven to influence others as quickly as possible without sacrificing quality in any way
- Eager to completely understand any idea or concept before bringing it before others
- Competitive and individualistic in his approach; prefers to work alone and maintain control of the process
- Diagnostic in approach; he asks probing questions, ascertains the problem, and applies a solution proven to work
- More comfortable answering questions or objections if he's had time to think about his response and can provide proof to support it.

MANAGEMENT STRATEGIES

To maximize his effectiveness, productivity, and job satisfaction, consider providing Jim with the following:

- Opportunities to broaden the technical knowledge of his work with learning experience in increasingly responsible positions.
- As much autonomy as possible in setting priorities, expressing his ideas, and putting them into action
- Recognition for tangible results obtained, rather than for political or selling skills
- Freedom from repetition
- Technical challenges to which he can apply innovative solutions.

Prepared by Richard Sweeney on 10/2/2014

81

The Final Chapter

You will have many final chapters in your life. The first one is leaving home, then school. Likely you will leave employers several times. Minimally, you will move from department to department and leave old colleagues behind. These are all final chapters.

You will be surprised how many final chapters crop up over the years. When a child suddenly grows up (do you realize they have spent half the time they are going to spend with you by the time they are in the fourth grade?). When a delightful overseas assignment ends. When your parents die. Perhaps you will lose a sibling. Tragically, you may lose a child. A beloved pet inevitably departs.

Ultimately, you will experience the final, final chapter yourself. Unless an accident overtakes you or you pass suddenly from a heart attack or similar body failure, in modern America you will likely experience this in a hospice center. If you have your faculties, that is you are not drugged to senselessness because of pain, you will have an opportunity to reflect on how you have done against plan, what it all means.

So, what is the difference between this happening at age 45, 65 or 85? When that day comes, all you will be left with is memories no matter your age. Perhaps twenty more years of great memories, at age 85, but perhaps not if you don't get past 65. You have no idea what might happen to you and your family in those twenty or forty years, shall we call them bonus years— they may be years of joy or they may be years of sorrow and debilitating misery—we just don't know. We foolishly think they will be years of joy, no matter our previous experiences.

It is in the human spirit to live on this earth as long as we can (some of us, through faith, have plans beyond living on this old rock). It is also in human nature to avoid thinking about the end. I hope I have given you some reasons, through a greater understanding of what you are engaged in right now in our industry, to think about the end a bit and, if necessary, adjust your path, no matter your current age or belief system, towards the goal of making those hospice reflections, which I hope you are privileged to experience way out in the future, to be ones with minimal regrets.

Live life honorably.

Live life to the fullest.

(cont'd from "what readers are saying...")

James V. Painter, Mt. Juliet, Tennessee

April 17, 2017

To: Mr. Jim Thompson

My name is Jim Painter, Vice President and General Manager, Retired.

I heartily endorse your new book outlining the leadership characteristics of paper business management. Hopefully, it will give some help to those struggling for success.

I started my career in the converting industry and spent a number of years with paper, plastic, metal and extruding businesses. I have always gone to paper mills that were in trouble the first one being purchased out of bankruptcy. My basic principles have always been, "Do The Right Thing, Because It Is The Right Thing To Do!" and "Treat People The Way You Want To Be Treated!" This works in every industry and business.

The first mill I was involved in had four light weight machines producing very high quality paper. They had been losing money for years and we got control of the mill on May 10 and made $350,000 that May by eliminating 80 employees and one customer who was buying the paper at the price of NBSK! Within three months we had the customer back at 45% margin.

My last position was at a closed [water system] recycled mill that was new but produced terrible quality

e

paper. When I retired the mill had very low costs and made excellent quality paper that was traded ton for ton with virgin linerboard and medium. The mill continues to be very successful today.

Obviously, I love challenges.

Early in my converting career I saw the cost to the company and the damage to the employees accidents caused so I became a Safety champion. I was a leader in random drug testing and terminating employees for unsafe acts. The latest statistics I have seen shows 96% of all accidents are from unsafe acts. When someone gets hurt and you shut the mill down for hours and have every employee at the mill on the investigating team it makes an impression! Employee Safety should always be the managers' and employees' number one priority! One mill I went to was averaging 20% of the employees with medical or lost time accidents a year. We ended up with years with no accidents. The bonus system penalized all employees significantly for any medical or lost time accidents.

All of my employee handbooks start out with, "Safety Takes Priority In All Activities!" and "No One Is Required To Perform Any Task That He/She Is Not Trained To Do Or Does Not Feel Comfortable Doing!" This puts safety right in the employees' lap. Management must believe this and live by it.

No one wants poor quality anything. Product quality must be the second most important goal of any manager. When your customers want your paper because it runs better and faster and makes higher quality products you get many, many calls for extra loads and very few frantic

f

customer calls. However, when customer complaints did occur top mill management went to the customer's plant the day of the call if possible. Why more mills don't do this I don't know. Keeping the customer happy should always be a top priority and keeps profits high. The mills I managed sold all the paper they could produce.

All the mills I have managed were losing money big time when I went to them. When I took my wife through one before I got involved she came out and said, "Why would anyone want to work there?' and "Only you would see the potential in that place!" Profitability is king for any business but to get there you must have high quality and dedicated employees. I have never seen an operation with bad employees, but I have seen tons with poor or bad management.

I strongly believe in bonus systems and sharing results with employees. Turning operations around by giving all employees authority to act and big bonuses develops a team that will run through walls for you. When an employee gets a $10,000-$15,000 bonus one year and it is not so much the next year everyone is disappointed including spouses. Fair bonus systems work wonders. Unfair or changing bonus systems cause much more harm than good.

Jim Thompson talked about a manager that when he heard about a new house or saw a new car that he, "Had" that employee. My feeling was when that happened the mill and the employee had been successful and I was very proud of both. I had monthly shift meetings with all employees always starting with Safety and covering mill results, issues and opportunities. My philosophy has always been when things are going bad provide support and help and when things are going good, that is the time to apply pressure. Employee turnover was almost nonexistent. I was always honest with all employees. An employee told me one time they called me the "Boogie Man" because I was the one guy that would walk up to anyone and tell them they had a booger hanging out of their nose. I don't remember ever doing that but I took it as a complement. I never missed taking food and drink to the mill employees on Thanksgiving and Christmas in appreciation for their working on those days.

I have had the great fortune of having great bosses, supervisors, and mentors. I have also had very supportive peers and employees. When you treat people the way you want to be treated it works for you as well. But, during my travels I have met some real losers in all categories and wonder how they keep their jobs.

I have seen managers and companies treat suppliers like dirt. I believe if you treat all with dignity and respect you get it back. Our mills got to test and then a leg up on many new inventions because the vendors wanted to work with us and there was mutual respect. Vendors were a very important part of our mill teams and we became friends with them and were loyal to them while always keeping a sharp eye on cost.

I have seen managers agonize over decisions to the point of losing opportunities or never making a decision. My position has always been, make the decision and then make that decision work!

I think it was a tremendous advantage to me to not have a papermaking background. I cannot tell you the number of times I was told, "That Won't Work!" because it had

h

been tried so many times before at other mills. *Quizzing and challenging employees is a golden tool if done correctly. I think there is a big advantage to managers not having papermaking backgrounds so they can question everything which gives rise to excellent solutions.*

All the mills I managed ended up with returns on investments well above industry averages.

Finally, I loved to play golf and race cars. You can still think about business on the golf course but you had better not be thinking about anything else but what you are doing at 180 MPH on a race track. Golf and racing were a great release for me.

My priorities in life have been my church, my family, and my job. However, my job almost always came first so I could have the other two!

Jim Painter

Made in the USA
Coppell, TX
09 September 2021

62077180R00059